I0201253

Cocaine Poems For a New Day

by

Leon Gratton

Grosvenor House
Publishing Limited

All rights reserved
Copyright © Leon Gratton, 2015

The right of Leon Gratton to be identified as the author of this
work has been asserted by him in accordance with Section 78
of the Copyright, Designs and Patents Act 1988

The book cover picture is copyright to Inmagine Corp LLC

This book is published by
Grosvenor House Publishing Ltd
28-30 High Street, Guildford, Surrey, GU1 3EL.
www.grosvenorhousepublishing.co.uk

This book is sold subject to the conditions that it shall not, by way of
trade or otherwise, be lent, resold, hired out or otherwise circulated
without the author's or publisher's prior consent in any form of binding or
cover other than that in which it is published and
without a similar condition including this condition being imposed
on the subsequent purchaser.

A CIP record for this book
is available from the British Library

ISBN 978-1-78148-480-7

Cocaine Poems for a New Day

Well the night slows down
My heart pounds
The only thing I ask is
That when shadows call
Make sure the children don't fall

Shadows moon
Shade of brilliance
Animal tomb

Time we awoke to the millions of stars
We behold as dreams
Quiet playful reversing into reality
The smile of the purest hearts
Braved and weighed night after night
With cold furrowing and nights of flight
Heaven opens up with a yawn and guardian
Angels come forth with years of armour made of gold

Sails

Mettle must be tried
By the unknown and settle quiet find
Where the soul finds resilience
And boasts it sails
And become Majestical lines
The beauty of our Immortal
Spirit sounds of in moon and sun
More power to the travelling Souls

He's one of those
Quiet, envoked explorers
Into the night
Into the night
Love peels back
Unassuming

Shared reason
Sunday Pray
Liquorice lips
With captive cocaine pay
The café that was Coca Cola
Turn to the rebel of strange way
Pray for reason
Pray with bones
Of narcotic slaves
Goodnight lady
The winter went away

Well sudden flash of light
In the underworld
Scribing passion and changing delight
The summer caution
And millions of graces of god
My lord jury of the weak
Go not into foolish sign
Dress my angel as the storm is
Nearly over
Lovers be still

Characters
Of some ancient
Night to be pulled
From half death
And taught how
To save a life

Paper tooth
Trying to solve the way
In sugar and liquid
We turn nice treats
To the street where
Acid of all minds
And should become
Delicate in love

Sugar kisses
And vampire bites
Love in disguise
Over filling passion
And creating night

If Indian summers
Were times of old
And travelling runners
Were stories told
The silence of whispers
And heroes so bold
The sands that blister
And love over gold
You may smile at hatred
As if you were a queen on
A darkened throne
My younger blood sister
Will seal you with bones

The religion in the haze
Longing of damnable days
When immortals walk
At night and all hallow
Of pristine light

My guarded, jaded love
One world
One life
My heart settling on the fringe
Of death
Creating love in a holy breath

Peering into souls
Asylum
With marching moving
Soldiers of the street wars
And quiet in times
Tomb with sand
Quiet honey
It's by your command

The mirror drinks up
The ceiling
Creating fire on the icicle thief
The body rest
Turns to heroes test

The signs for time
Trapped in mysterious
calculation
And power of Bards ruination
Farewell fond deceiver
Open one eye
Open the other
Love lights up casual wonder

The lion at midnight
Wandering at, showing strength
The mind of jungle wisdom

Society a tomb

Society is a tomb
And narcotics, its womb
With raving, craven addicts of lust
It's as simple as forgetting trust
No-one likes the cold numb weather
And angels weigh their hearts against a feather
Girls and women all beautiful on this earth
Whilst man serves up evil at what it's worth
Rings on fingers
Are what they seem
Rings on fingers
Mean the earth to me
Couples hold hands
And the world turns with sands
Dawn with her radiance
Rings on fingers
But they somehow seem false

Why is the story
Never the same
Why is it a sickly poison
And dying in vain

I hope someday to live the life
of a thousand
Butterflies
Floating endlessly in the
summer haze
I hope someday to be the
noon tides
Wonder
And leave the white sands
in the suns
Ablaze
I hope someday to be the shadows
on the moon
And somehow see the kittens spoon

I Wonder

Conform to the Path
When together we laugh and laugh
The night creatures hear my words
It's quiet in time's womb
And I know ways of golden
dragons room
If in the thought of a smiling
generation
Utter insanity of degradation
I wonder at my words
I wonder
I wonder

The lust
The love
The quiet condemnation
You are wonders to beset
Caged in hearts
Minus the regret

Angel in a Storm

———∞∞∞———

Angel in a storm
With knights of Death
And blood red thorns
The quiet ones brooding
Where nothing is normal
And I see chapters of red
And men grow moody
The people come to the tree
And tides start soothing
That angel in a storm
Hot flame dropping onto ice
Melting through that
invisible time
And hell bleeds at
Christ-like
Thorns
We sin to begin to
settle our
Paths at ease
And there came an angel
in a storm

———∞∞∞———

The Holy Houses

The holy houses, goodbye
fellow Friend
The comatose whining of dark
departed trend
Cold, cold weather police the
ones who kill
And understand that no man
goes through
The time stands still
Bye woman large and unfair
Bye star of darkness with my
woman so fair

Broken Sky

The sun, the clouds in a broken sky
The time, the hourglass in a broken sky
The mind, the seeds in a broken sky
The world, it bleeds in a broken sky
The prisons, the shelter lead to a broken sky
The creatures, strange in a broken sky
The cheats, the lies shall all come undone
In a broken sky
The love, the sighs cry out each day
In a broken sky

Dream Maker

Tower Of Princes
Well of wishes bring me mine
To love and behold a beauty divine
Tower of princes, show me a way
To be true in love, and never sway
Women of wisdom, be so still
So I never forget, to bend to her will
Soldier of war, help me out
So I make a living, and her
I never forget about

Dream Maker

I wonder
I wonder
If in deep times we slumber
The dragon
The dragon
I sleep on seven summers
A vampire old cold
Lives at night
Cold and fallen for

Skulls

Skulls in the archive to live
confusion
Bones of the earth is mankind merely a
delusion
Sick in taste with our very
maiden sky
Tricked in confusion, the wings are
very high
We'll stretch to the limit, the skulls
in the earth
The child so fragile does ever
feel his birth

Morphine Cloth

A dusty cough
With morphine cloth
Take me to quiet waters
With sun and moon
The Texas wasp
Cloudy yet glowing
Moon trapped moth
The more I see her
The more I think of
Morphine Cloth

Pillow Case Eyes

Pillow case eyes
Moon drop disguise
With stars parading the skies
And hiding our souls the sun does
We go from strength to courage
Chasing away our hidden lies
Courage my friends in the art of combat
It's as subtle as watching an acrobat
Things close to the pitch night
Hide fair samurai from the sun

The Quiet Queen

Smooth as silk
Droplets of pure milk
Coffee brown eyes
Still I remember her
Hair burning red
Flowing down her shoulders
Oh how the embers
smoldered

Moonlight spheres
Cold dying sun
Reptilian dried skin
What becomes shall become
Cold cup of caffeine
You are my one
We take sail on a furious
driven sun
I love them all, my
precious one

Monsters of time

My heart cracked and bled
Surely heaven isn't just in the head
Other worlds we become
We are all chosen ones
Except those that kill in the
name of greed
Monsters of time
Whilst we try to soothe their minds
If the world is a veil
And the heroes never fail
Then that theme cannot be outdone
Closer to madness
Is the world of sadness
Which the monsters of time
Feed on

Sad Tuesday

Sad Tuesday, my heart a small flickering
flame
Sad Tuesday, the start of my way into the
narcotics game
Sad Tuesday, the people as well as me are
all insane
Sad Tuesday, the narcotics did I make it
plain
Sad Tuesday, after Monday's speed chase
we slept all day

It's only with love the heart and soul wants
The small brutal bruising of the heart
My consideration, yes time wept a small
poisonous tear

It's a world of heroes
And a million ways we shatter
The final way of pitter patter
My heart open but it doesn't matter
The rain on demons in hell
My way with platinum rolled shell

The night so young
Quietly gone to life so blunt
My well-wishing for someone so young
Misplaced
Disgraced
Over-intimidated
Well played
This street game
My tears a well of salt
No child
No child
Chaos is not your fault

Poets have souls that empires abound

Fever tonight
She's in the distance
But still in my second sight
I hope she meets no resistance
As I see an angel in flight

Mr Sinister

Crazy in love with someone up above
Love in truth it comes and goes
Raven-haired with gypsy eyes
She truly lives in loves disguise
Eyes beyond belief
And never mind heartfelt resentment
and relief
They should remember souls collide
all the time
Not a knot giving rhyme
Feelings destroyed
Heart broken
Words shall remain unspoken
Tokens of resentment
She would love to see a fight
It's not a delight to see blood
Ancients brood up above
Gods, angels, saints and ministers
Clear a path, I've just met Mr Sinister

The knight in armour
With firefly burning crows glamour
Turning arrows to powder
War a beautiful sight "Pah"
Silence, peace, treat those diseased
Make love, create don't desecrate
And be sure Mother Nature isn't a whore

Tho' my heart beats for you
You can't be with me, why?
Summer is almost gone
A darling of nature
I miss you like a dragon
misses its slumber
Gold coin, I love you
Magical ring, I love you
Endless gem, I love you
Deck of many things, I love you
Heaps of blessings, I'll cry with you
A fitting end to the prince of dragons

Old creatures sitting in the dying light
When colours fade into the neon light
The subtle beauty sullen stone
Runs with blonde
And loves to the bone
I will seize his empire
I will love over the throne
Scribe in the tribe
With quiet ringing of the phone
She has it all
Man alive I'd have a ball
Codeine, pethidine, and of
course morphine

Heart pounding in the distance
A river of moonlight beams
The distance of love on cherry streams
Gone twilight, morning suns
A plateau of love that never comes
My love is a sunlight tale
And heaven in its attitude never shall fail

Love talk on a moon so high
Love talk that leaves you to sigh
Love talk as I think about her inner thigh
Love talk to the one in blue
Love talk through and through
Love talk yes it's got to be true
Love talk in strange man's head
Love talk silken thread
Love talk passion we carefully tread
Love love love

The night runs silent
And vampires are on my mind
Silver steak on a break
Food is what I mean
Food for thought
A vampiric touch is hot
Quiet now
Hush up
Cuddle lovers
Be the true other
Half in the craft of love

The world in the middle
Cards turn
Wonder is the riddle
Never will we burn
Love is what I seek
Pairs of lovers who silently speak
I see you there more beauty
I would turn to you and do
any duty

Night of menace I watch
a rose
She is beauty in
a trance

The night smiles and moons sway
As black holes come after our sun
Why must we become nothing after death
They know nothing
Bye cancerous breath
Shallow howling wind
We turn up and the opiate
Cocaine trade starts again
Feign deeply insane
Venus, is she that desperate
Mars are you that vain
Explosion in Christ warm summer rain
In here she says
But the nightmares won't go away

The night only saves
But day gentle day
Shows us how hard the gods worked
The silent man contemplates
Whether his love is worthy of a temptress
My lord the love he wants is never far
He just has to look
I wonder if Janice remembers me
Woman of true love I called out to you
My heart is battered, broken and blue
If they can't see Canticle
Then they have destroyed both Dawn
And sailing night

In spring, wilderness sings
In night, life gives us a fright
In morn, chariots of peace adorn
In our love, we pray to above
In our passion, we live in and out
Of fashion
In the smile, we wait a while
I miss you
Starlight wonder
Do you remember that summer
I made a mistake
Then died a depth in a vampires wake
etc.....

The perfection seems invaluable
But countless have seen the insoluble
No way of putting it but a
Hundred, thousand depths of emotion
Fear, desire, love, agitation, angst
Sorrow etc.......

Alright

The customary final decision
Left with time to think on proposition
Final demands flood our floors
The music forever timeless has got
To be the doors
The rhythmic keyboard playing in the
March cool air
The baritone going to sombre midday
Word man, spy and lover of wine
Keep the mystique unique. Keep rolling
Along the highway and steal the deal
Until it becomes unreal

Pit bull borstals

The final thought I wonder what
It'll be, will it be joyful of the
release.
Will it be of heaven.
God damn this disease.
Ease into the tomb
Society numb
We act like blind deaf
madmen
And silently dumb
Deep thinkers are shallow
Whilst pit bull borstals
Are on the run
The privileged get it easy
And I settle on a cold
dying sun.

Dragons blood

———⊗⊗⊗———

The daunting feeling
Yes tears again
My world trance-like
With happiness spilling from the
Pen.
Quiet in summer
Trance like I wonder
If the smell of ecstatic
Nights the bottle had a genie
In it. I will burn the smart
Incense and wonder why she was
Left with dragon's blood
My servants are drowning
Slowly in boredom
And a genuine close call
She was there but none fall
What have I done?

———⊗⊗⊗———

Pear Tree

⸺∞⸺

Pear tree summer
The more I love her the more I wonder
I'm not in it for the money
As everyone knows you sell your soul for that
The sylph came again. So many warnings
So many dawnings they keep hurting me
So tell me how long must I keep up
With this scene
I'm leaving
No wonder

⸺∞⸺

Dark Star

The people wander in and out
Twisting this place of confusion
My heart honest and fair
The people petty I wonder what's out
There.
Quietly the music plays
Games in the midnight air
I'm lonely nearly in tears.
She treats me warm then treats me cold
Dark star
Dark star
Tell me what you think
The colour of the season
I won't tell you I'll let you
Think.

Sugartooth

It's a sad sweet moment
Which stays in my heart
The day we parted
Was the day I cried
But I smile at your heartache
As I know it's the same as mine
Your love got me started
In this soul filled mine
And now we've parted
I hope you'll keep me in mind
I reach across a country
And hope you'll be mine
I got some time for tenderness
And I hope you feel the same
I smile at the wonderment
And cry at what we've gained
And you know since we parted
That loves a lullaby

Moon and Stars

Tree of life
For your wife
Piercing of flesh
But not by a knife
Needles of paint
To mark my time
Neither shall shudder
Neither shall scar
Moon and stars

There's something amazing
About this world
Where we become
Tragic in the politics
Of society
We apologise politely
Pose silently in a calm, resolute way
Women, wine and narcotic sleep
The love I have I will
Always keep

I have become lazy
These days
Frankly the care for
Nothing in this world
But all is sought after
The temperature is
Breaking me

Only once when the moon
Becomes nobler in the inky
Black skies
And we become a small
Speck of stardust
Living in the astral
Plane of dark night
It's our free will
Closing in to make a stand
For heaven

I am a scribe
Wandering lonely in this tribe
The Jesus in me to awake and subscribe
To the lunatic moon
Wailing, moping, morning sun
Becomes wanting paradise which
we become

The lust
The love
The quiet condemnation
You are wonders to beset
Caged in hearts
Minus the regret

White Poppy Dreams

Silence booms with bones
Quiet shhh move the loans
We watch for sharks
On the desert of dangerous Tomes
We know the brilliance of kings
And queens
Move posture
Move to the scenes
White poppy
Seen the scars
The prospect of dying in dreams
Bye to sullen dry wit
My heart loves white poppy dreams

Cocaine candy
And kissing clowns
We rock back
And walk back
From a darker side of town

My hero has left
My heroine made quiet love to me
Over the precious souls we have

Sweetness refined
Open to conscious space
Love hope lips like sugar
Please me with tender kiss
The opiate sea we crossed
Left many wise men, we lost
The pain of heartache
Comes with celestial twist
My sound of hurt killing
My heart and soul

A million kisses
Which all feel and taste sweet
The universe which gods made
Has left me in love
Going on the trip
That which makes my heart skip
Makes my soul flip
Becomes a natural flow
And slip
Love shines on

It's months since I pled
Guilty in the universe's
courtroom
To the sound of lovers
Buying their way out of sin
Bored of nights with stars
Flowing in bursts of powder lights

Soul Food

The space I give
Whilst the life you live
I'm a sorrowful heart
Please remember the start
Quiet I wait
Wondering whether you'll
love me soon
It's granted your words
In the hope of love
Traced in my eyes heavens above
But no one believes in poetic slaves
They think it's set to graves
With music reflecting our very mood
Love in the kitchen set to soul food

Children of the rain

True I've come to this place over and over again
Where silence sleeps in time and in pain
Promise I will love you without the
greyness and insane
Tho' love will show you why we are
children of the rain
And blue skies continue to be shallow in their way
And somehow I miss you on a fateful day

Who is this queen of dreams?
Who dusts me with diamonds
And sets me free
Who is this woman of gentle cool night
Who summons silence
And shows me what's right
Who is this angel of blue
Who has secret entry
And loves me true
Starry-eyed and wondrous
A smile on her face
One of gladness
And kindness
An angel in this race

Starry eyed and restless
She lives with cocaine grace
The smile that adorned her
Has been put away safe

Pinholes shining
In the dark satin cloth
Of death that wraps
Around us
The world turns
And silently we endure
The love of life
And small allure
Its lustre gone
The gold in sands
That turn with each
Lapping wave

It's time she says
Smiling proudly
At winter gem
Ghosts move thru'
This world
Hurting as we die

My way of seeing
Thru' this storm
Is cruel and angry
My heart turned
Black with confusion and lies
The small decency came
Not from a loved one
But at caring deep in my
Heart for everyone

Some ways are indivisible
The Wild West
The Far East
A genuine man
A good man
Will take on the fact
That when you save
A life you become responsible for it

Opium pipes smile
And sweet poppy
Wafts away my cares
Honey has treacle in the smiling trade
A dealer
A true gentry
In the poppy days

The family man
Gambling when he can
Sullen open hours
Fear of the towers
Devils playground
That's what they call west
Edinburgh
Don't have a clue
Watch your own
Back see what they do

The silent feast for none but the few
You are hurt with ecstatic tinge
And only want which is not for
wanting's sake
Honey no need for the money
Your miracle is you
Thru' and thru'
Such a woman true and true

Well quiet mistakes
I never fake
The feeling the passion
The night the fashions
You are a goddess
And tears I weep
Sometimes I wonder
If angels like you and I
Take with passion and make love
In the sky
The stars, ancient. I love you madly

—∞—

Hopeless chanting
Tiger feet
If you miss me
Say so
It hurts and I'm sorry
Even if you hate me
It must be out of love
So don't worry
Your smile shines thru'
And no matter what
we've done
I'll love you true

—∞—

A kiss please gentle on the cheek
Did I say you are all ladies
And my heart rushes and pulse slows
Down
To verbal insults
A huntsman, tracker with Morrison
In his blood
His sniff but you never need insist
I pick up a voice on the breeze
Summon my family and become
Intrigued
Elementary he'd arrest the wrong one
Sleep, dream, I believe in Kingdom come
Worlds

The night smiles and moons sway
As black holes come after our sun
Why must we become nothing
After death
They know nothing
Bye to cancerous breath
Shallow howling wind
We turn up and the opiate cocaine
Trade starts again
Feign, deeply insane
Venus, is she that desperate
Mars are you that vain
Explosion in Christ warm summer
Rain
In here she says
But the nightmares won't go away

Well I know things
Quiet as the beat of cherubs' wings
The sullen high priestess sings
My world of love can mount away
And Psyche and Aphrodite come
And stay
Unknown with worlds I play
And play
Nurture my dearest of people
And sound my numerous graves
The lovers' amazement with gods
Kingdom come
Truth forbidden and loved by some

No! You say. Then why did I ask
You mock green demons and deadly
Jesters
Sister you may think I've no
Love to give
The tireless prose of fools
The gold moment of quiet plays
Why did you ask
If it was a turning point?

Well I don't see a fool
I see a man envenomed by bitter
Tongues and utter nasty stairs
The release you need is a
Volume of the quiet volume
The tome of inseparable ways
The thanking of crimes when
Forced into shadows of night
Sword for a slave

Maybe I'm the blue-eyed devil
Ready to take your soul
Am I in love again
It's a renewable inexhaustible source
That can't be measured by anything
The moon and stars count every time
People fall in love
Do we muse on a sun
Do we muse on stars, the moon
Do we muse on dawn's tide turning
Am I the blue-eyed devil

I watch a quiet blue moon
Settle for breakneck tomb
Quiet brilliant
From a tattooed wound
We smile at Lizard men
And pretty cold set ways

Brown Sugar eyes
Soft and white
Sugar to touch
The art of love
Comes round
The whizz and stoney
Walk hand and hand
With principal
And enquiring sand

───◦◦◦───

Wintertime rain
Cold and freezing
Shows us the world is truly
bleeding
Glad we are in glowing houses
Where love and fashion shows us
warmth
Night crawls in
When women dress warm
And love comes and stays
Quietly I think of wintertime rain
Where comfort and passion
Steal us away

Peel

The moon in its way
Sends me forth on the sea's lapping sway
The love I feel is blind and turned
My heart melted I could easily peel
With valium or benzedrine so that I no longer feel
The drugs I did were unreal
In the fact that I no longer beg, borrow or steal
I'm in habitual thoughts
Bringing forth psychosis that
I haven't been taught
My world blood, wounds since childhood
Am I always going to be the addict
With a doctor's way and a script
These poisons that I've sipped
Alone I'd be as well cooking up a bone
And leaving this world forever
But then I look at dawn and see the
night gently fade
Hell I destroyed a ring of night shade
As much as I believe
There are other ways to receive
Love, tenderness and prayer
The many mused musings

Girls Who Say

Watching the reflection in the mirror
Hoping my inner reason shows it better
Slow to behold an end to the cold grey weather
With spring in mind
The angelic wings feathered
Blood from the wound
Just below the triangle
Golden womb
Looking carefully, societies tomb
Where pitiful rest with closed
Eyes and a cheerful guest
Inner depth
With a day at best
I still taste the salt
From a tequila morning
The headache dropped and left
No warning
Jack and Jills
No time to thrill
Quietly I come out no wonder
I'm under the weather
Her kiss pure and now my life severed
Her kiss so sweet was I really dreaming of leather
Old in ways
Girls who say
I love you

www.ingramcontent.com/pod-product-compliance
Lightning Source LLC
Chambersburg PA
CBHW021221020426
42331CB00003B/413